DID YOU KNOW?
Penguins

DID YOU KNOW?

Penguins

young reed

Contents

What is a Penguin?

Gentoo Penguin adult and chick.

● Penguins are a family of flightless birds.
Although they have wings and feathers, these are
superbly adapted for swimming through the ocean.

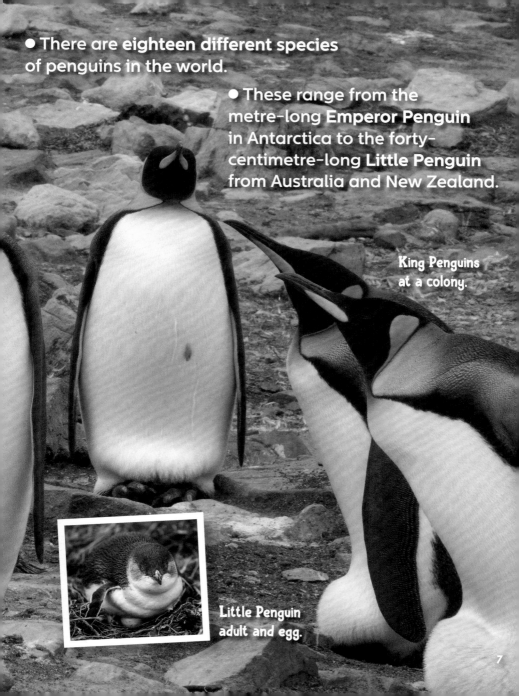

● There are **eighteen different species** of penguins in the world.

● These range from the metre-long **Emperor Penguin** in Antarctica to the forty-centimetre-long **Little Penguin** from Australia and New Zealand.

King Penguins at a colony.

Little Penguin adult and egg.

Amazing adaptations

- Their streamlined torpedo-like shape and flipper wings help penguins to swim super-fast — it's almost as if they are flying through the water.

...waterproof **plumage**.

● All species are dark above and white below — this is a type of **camouflage** called **countershading** that helps to hide swimming penguins from predators.

● Penguin **bones** are **heavier** than those of other birds, to help make swimming underwater easier.

Young African Penguin moulting from down to adult plumage.

Galápagos Penguin.

Where do Penguins live?

- Today, captive penguins are a familiar sight in **zoos** an **animal parks** all around the world, where they have become a favourite attraction for millions of people.

- In the wild, however, penguins live in the world's **southern oceans**, from icy Antarctica to the tropical waters around the Galápagos Islands, close to the Equator.

- Many penguin species only come to land to breed. The birds often spend many months at a time at sea.

King Penguin colony.

Family life – Penguin cities

● Penguins nest together in **colonies**. Sometimes these are enormous and spectacular, for example the King and Emperor Penguins that nest in the open with thousands of birds seeming to stand shoulder to shoulder.

● These large penguins nest in cold climates. Rather than build a nest, the adult will balance the egg or young chick on its feet in order to keep it warm. The adult has a **brood patch** to help with incubation.

Adult brooding egg.

The brood patch.

Adult King Penguin feeding young.

African Penguins nesting in a loose colony.

- Other penguin species nest in scattered colonies, hiding their eggs and young in tangles of tree roots, among rocks or even in specially made **nest boxes**.

- Some species dig a **nest burrow** in the soil.

- The adult penguins feed the chicks on a fishy paste that they **regurgitate** from their stomachs — delicious!

Little Penguin in nest box.

What's for dinner?

● **Fish,** and lots of it! Although other marine animals such as **squid** and **krill** also feature on the menu.

● Penguins can swim fast in bursts – up to **forty kilometres per hour** – in pursuit of their quarry.

● To catch their prey penguins can dive to depths of up to **five hundred metres** and stay submerged for **twenty minutes** – that's a deep breath!

Getting around

● Penguins are famously graceful in water but awkward on land — looking comical to our eyes with their **waddling** walk.

● Some penguins that nest in Antarctica travel long distances by sliding — or **tobogganing** — across the ice on their bellies.

Emperor Penguins tobogganing.

● Although officially flightless, penguins can take to the air in two ways — the first is by jumping or **rockhopping**. In fact there are two species of penguins called Rockhoppers.

Fiordland Penguin jumping.

● When a penguin is swimming fast it can break the surface of the water and glide like a dolphin. This is known as **porpoising**.

Chinstrap Penguin porpoising.

Penguins in peril

- Natural predators of adult penguins include **seals**, **sharks** and **Orcas**.

● Gulls, foxes and birds of prey can eat their eggs and chicks.

● Humans add further pressure to penguin populations due to issues such as **plastic waste** and **global warming**.

Record breakers

● In prehistoric times there were giant penguins measuring up to **two metres** tall — that's twice the length of today's Emperor Penguins.

Emperor Penguins.

Chinstrap Penguin colony.

● Sub-Antarctic Zadovski Island is home to the world's largest penguin colony. It holds more than **one million** Chinstrap Penguins.

● The temperature at an Emperor Penguin colony can reach **minus forty degrees**, with winds of more than **one hundred and forty kilometres per hour**.

First published in 2025 by
New Holland Publishers
Sydney

newhollandpublishers.com

Level 1, 178 Fox Valley Road, Wahroonga, NSW 2076, Australia

A record of this book is held at the National Library of Australia.

ISBN 978 1 92107 390 8

OTHER TITLES IN THE 'DID YOU KNOW?' SERIES:

Kangaroos
ISBN 978 1 92107 386 1

Koala
ISBN 978 1 92107 387 8

Lizards
ISBN 978 1 92107 388 5

Meerkat
ISBN 978 1 92107 389 2

Red Panda
ISBN 978 1 92107 391 5

For details of these books and hundreds
of other Natural History titles see
newhollandpublishers.com